TO APPLY A
TATTOO

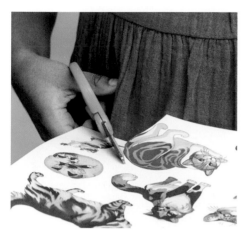

1 Cut out the tattoo and remove the plastic cover.

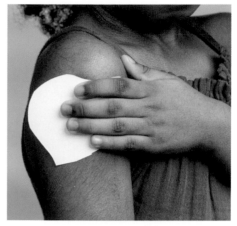

2 Stick the tattoo, picture-side down, onto clean, dry skin.

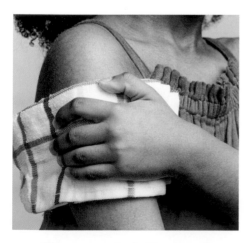

3 Place a wet cloth over the tattoo. Press down gently for about 30 seconds. Hold it still!

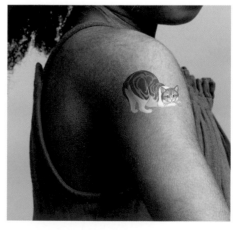

4 Gently slide off the paper backing. Do not touch until it's dry.

TIP: To remove tattoos, dab with rubbing alcohol or baby oil. Wait 10 seconds, then rub gently. Apply more rubbing alcohol or baby oil repeatedly until removed.

ABYSSINIAN ➤

The Aby, as it's affectionately called, is one of the oldest known cat breeds. These friendly, curious, and intelligent cats like to know what's going on around them.

◄ AMERICAN SHORTHAIR

With a thick, soft coat and a gentle nature, American shorthairs make wonderful family pets. Tabby is the most common coat pattern, but they can be all white or black, calico, tortoiseshell, or one of more than 80 other coat and color combinations.

BENGAL ➤

Bengals look like little leopards or jaguars, with their beautifully spotted fur. They are active, energetic cats who enjoy being part of a family.

◄ BRITISH SHORTHAIR

These sturdy, cuddly cats have plush fur and big, round eyes. They are large and easygoing.

Cats extend their claws when they want to catch prey or defend themselves. Sometimes you can see their claws when they are stretching.

DEVON REX ▼

Some people think Devon rexes look a little like aliens, with their crinkly fur, big eyes, and large triangular ears.

MIXED-BREED CATS ▾

Most cats aren't any particular breed. Cats are found all over the world in every color. They can be big or small, and they can have short or long hair.

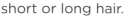

Stroke cats from head to tail. Going the other way ruffles their fur, which cats don't like.

◄ EXOTIC SHORTHAIR

Exotics look like fancy Persians but without all the fluff. They are sweet, quiet cats who love to snuggle.

MAINE COON ▼

Maine coons are among the largest of cats, with some males weighing as much as 20 pounds! These gentle giants come in all colors and have tufted ears.

MANX ➤

A cat with no tail? Yes, that's the way Manx cats are born. This ancient breed from the Isle of Man was shown in the first cat show held in Great Britain in 1871.

◄ PERSIAN

These lovable balls of fluff with their round faces and smushed-in noses are one of the most popular breeds in the world.

RAGDOLL ⌄

These big, beautiful cats with bright blue eyes are known for being affectionate and outgoing. They love to cuddle and need less brushing than some other longhaired breeds.

SCOTTISH FOLD ➤

With their folded ears, round faces, and big eyes, these cats look like owls. They are said to be good-natured and affectionate.

SIAMESE ▾

This unique breed is easy to identify, with its dark "points" (ears, muzzle, paws, and tail) and its striking blue eyes. Siamese cats are known for being vocal.

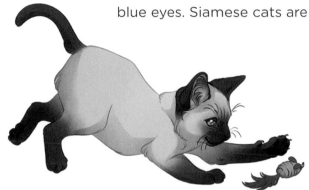

Cats purr when they are happy and relaxed. They sometimes purr when they are afraid, perhaps to comfort themselves.

SPHYNX ➤

Developed from a kitten born in 1966, the sphynx breed is naturally hairless. They are playful and like to interact with people.

Tuxedo, tabby, calico, and tortoiseshell are coat colors, not breeds. Some breeds, like the American shorthair, can be a variety of colors, including these four. Other breeds, like the Siamese, come in fewer colors.

▼ TUXEDO

A tuxedo cat is mostly black with white markings. Some of them look like they're wearing fancy suits!

TABBY ➤

The tabby pattern can be found in many different breeds. Coats can be striped, swirly, or spotted, and come in many colors. Many tabbies have a color pattern on their forehead that resembles the letter *M*.

Tabby cats are so common that many people refer to all cats as "tabbies."

CALICO ➤

A calico cat's coat is a combination of black, orange, and white. Each one is different!

Calico and tortoiseshell cats are almost always female.

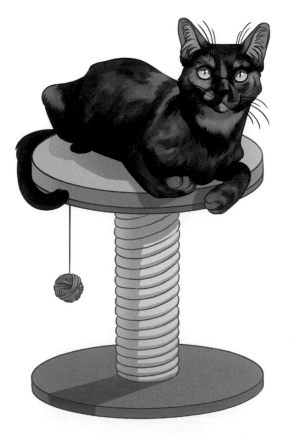

◄ TORTOISESHELL

These cats have coats that mix two colors, such as orange and black or gray, with very little or no white markings. There might be distinct splotches of color, or the colors might be swirled together.